this way, a bed is waiting for you

Corinne Hackett

BookLeaf
Publishing

India | USA | UK

Presentation by *BookLeaf Publishing*

Web: www.bookleafpub.com

E-mail: info@bookleafpub.com

ISBN: 9789360944872

First edition 2024

For everyone who woke up this morning.

ACKNOWLEDGEMENT

Firstly, thank you to whoever is reading! I hope I was able to keep you company for a little while, and hopefully I made you smile. Thank you so dearly to BookLeaf for this incredible opportunity. You made my little writer dreams come true.

I really want to thank my parents. Mum, the entire world would be healed from one of your hugs. Dad, thank you for every caramel latte and singing Disney songs in the car. I would be nothing without you both. Thank you to my two sisters - I can only dream of being half of the women you both are.

Thank you to my friends! My blankets in the cold. A special thank you to Christian, Leo, Emilia, Gary, Marthe and Emma. This chapter of life was extremely challenging, and you special souls held me together when I was crumbling. I will forever be in your debts.

An even more special thank you to Sidney. I can't capture your brilliance in words, so thank you for giving me a love I cannot describe. You are my heart's safety net.

And lastly, thank you to little me, who never gave up.

Goodnight for now.

Corinne x

PREFACE

These poems discuss heavy themes such as
self-injury, implications of suicide and
descriptions of anxiety.
Keep yourself safe. Sending lots of love.

prelude

What a warm, trembling welcome.
I have met many bathroom floors
this way.

Toes twisting,
Knees knocking,
Tears slopping into
Tired teeth.
I curl into anything but
a bed.

I pop open my basilic vein,
our special bubbly.
Glasses are raised to those
who succeed.
I will sleep soon.
The bathtub
is waiting.

I think of my mother.
she drinks her tea
next door,
with the dog in her lap.
The house is still, at last.
This is all
for you.

It is a scene
painfully overripe.
It gets a chuckle
out of me.
It stops me,
and makes me realise
I must write about it tomorrow.

And there it is.

And here you are,
holding my worst
and bending my spine.
I hope I treat your eyes with care.
If you see me,
or you,
or someone you once knew.

Let us treat each other gently.

this little dog

This little dog will be spoiled
on her last day with me.

I gave her a rosy sunrise
with an extra hour of sleep.

She had chocolate for breakfast
and didn't brush her teeth.

She laced up her favourite converse,
the ones with sunflowers underneath.

This little dog loved the woods,
so to the woods we went.

I held up flowers on her way,
but she never took in their scent.

She sat alone in her favourite tree,
and I leant against her side.

I wish she knew I was there,
maybe then, she would not have cried.

This little dog went home,
and I lit up the dirt.

The house was quiet.
I prayed it wouldn't hurt.

With a note in her hand,
and no more wags in her tail,

This little dog went into the bathroom
with a heart feeling stale.

I made the world furious for her,
the sky opened up to a tear.

Thank you for spending a little time with me,
friend.
May there be peace elsewhere.

kalopsia

I wake up
without a jolt.
Sunlight drips through the blinds
like honey,
into my heart of honeycomb.

The morning is darling company.
She makes me coffee
and we sit on a balcony,
or a couch,
or beside a sleeping love.
Maybe there's a cat sprawled on the porch.
There is a pile of shoes at the door
and it feels so right.
Wind chimes are humming.
The day feels soft on my skin.

Today, I will fold my laundry
and watch movies that let me
catch a glimpse of it.
Maybe I'll do a cartwheel.

I was pushed into life,
kicking and screaming.

I meet the bathroom floor
the same way.

Hope stands in the doorway.
she is the biggest fool
I've ever known.
I hope her screaming ceases.
I hope I realise she's right.

I hope I meet this morning.

mosaic

I watch you
from the corner
of a stranger's living room.

You laugh at jokes
dripping in harm.

I've always hated honest people.
That's why I liked you.

You dance around your mother's guilt
and call it home.
You are pulling someone by the waist,
a devilish air to your angel face.

You slide a can across the counter
and I see a child
slide a juice cup.
A move my father taught you.

What went wrong?
Who went wrong?
Perhaps I went wrong.

I am wrong
in being here.

Parties teach me this best.

I am an approval-addicted machine.
I swallow my vomit
and condemn it to alcohol poisoning.

Your friends slur their praise into my lips
and I want to wail.

I fade away into the confession chamber
of a fresher's bathroom
and pray in retches
to Gods I do not believe in.

In picking up the pieces of the you
I once knew,
I found the new you
budding in me.

Please undo the mess that is me,
that is us.

Please, God.

saturn and her rings

Saturn is giving up soon.

The slam of earth's door ripples through her
core.
Telescopes brush past her. She is the youngest
sibling under a parent's camera.
Pluto smiles at her every thirty years.
Pluto is lying every thirty years.
She will never stop asking Pluto how she does it.
'You'll never need to know,' says Pluto. 'You're
Saturn.'
Saturn nods.
When she is out of Pluto's sight, she wails.

Saturn is giving up soon.

She spent a hundred bloodlines nurturing halos
around her body,
floating silk within stars.
The cosmos sat, chins in palms,
watching them weave a life -
a bond which time turned her back to,
as she knows it would surpass her.
She caught meteor showers
so the stars never felt a drizzle.

Saturn was brave enough to declare war against
fate.
Saturn was naïve enough to believe she'd win.

Saturn is giving up soon.

She can't remember when her rings
drooped,
like an older sister's cardigan she forgot is
stolen.
She doesn't remember her rings being dust.
She will never remember her rings being dust.
She will never forget that day,
feeling her liquid core,
remembering no one's footprints will stay.

Saturn is giving up soon.

Thirty years have passed,
her teeth chatter.
The way Pluto looks at her runs her blood cold.
Too close to a mirror.
Time is nowhere to be seen
to heal her gaping wounds.
She'll spend her days stitching wounds
she earnt while stitching wounds.

If fate has a slither of grace left in her bones,

maybe Saturn walks into a coffee shop
and drops a napkin at the feet of her rings,
or holds the door open for her,
or stands under the same moon as her,
and she can see her dimples again,
and welcome her home again,
and ask time to pretend she never saw them
again,

And they will start again.

Now,
Saturn gives the past to the future
as a present.
She flicks one last comet away.

Saturn survives.

even a worm will turn

As I write these words,
I breathe in shakes.

Today, I will try to find the strength
to be angry.

Burdens are heaviest
when they are silent.

Muscles are easily bruised,
when

I let you hurt me
so I didn't have to.

I took my dusty heart out
for you,
for you to leave her
frightened
in hotel rooms.
Like a lost toy,
She squeaked for help -
how dare she forget
your working hours were over.

I sucked in my shoulders

curdled my organs
twisted my spine
and crossed my legs over
the side of every chair
at every dinner.
A man's ego
needs table room.

Is a bruised ego that awful?
Is the bruise so bright and prodding and ripe
it distracts you in the mirror
from your own actions?

Only one of us is distracted.
The other has grown repulsed
by the stench of dirty laundry.

My soft heart
is not a naïve one -
your first mistake.
Kind women are not cleaners -
second mistake.

I'm busy having my shoulders massaged
to air your dirty laundry,
charmed and airy.

I have poured poison into your future
but you have turned mine into diamonds.

bubble wrap

I wish I was made from bubble wrap.
Something that cradles your fragile
and will not let it fall.

I wish to hug your snow globe,
even for a season.
She will never know
how to be cold.

I wish to be the joy
in fragile parcels.
I wish to be the handle
of care.

I wish bubble wrap
could protect glass
that is already broken.

I wish I was not naïve enough
to try.

I'll cushion your pain
with my open wounds.
I will,
I will, I will,

until there is shattered glass covering the floor
and I cannot scream.

This is the breaking of me.
I wish I was not built to protect everything,

When I cannot.

if the dancefloor could talk

Tell me
you are waltzing somewhere.

Tell me those slippers are still as
curiously darling and kind
as I remember.
Tell me your hair still scrapes
into a bun
and the worst thing in your world
is ripped tights.

We haven't met
in a while.

Our last dance
was full of shaky ankles
and thumping heels.

Tell me your ankles are strong.
Tell me you still float on relevé
under kitchen lights
and pirouette with your sister.

Tell me I'm hearing things
when your satin slippers

sound sour from
hospital floors
and your bun
is blocked
with tubes.
Tell me you'll greet my good friend
in the west of London.

I promise I'll look away
if you make a mistake.

Darling,
if our sweet reunion never comes,
please know
our pas des deux
will forever be the lift
to your smile.

Your laughter will hold the world under its arm
and spin it dizzy.

Never let your curtain fall,
friend.

a semester's act

One day,
maybe someday,
I'll leave my parents in the car,
carry my suitcases in alone,
and smile.

One day,
maybe today,
The girl who had to be
heaved off her mother in nursery
will not scoff at me.

Here she is.
clinging to her mother's hip.
Her dad can only say these will be
the best days of her life.

I don't believe him.
I am a child that needs tucked in.
I am a child who cannot
butter her own toast.
I am a child who loves to play pretend,

so my parents reverse
and take me back in their arms.

I am not pushed to stare my own life
in the face
for the first time
just yet.
I am nineteen, and know my life well.
I do not hide from the cold.
It does not find me in the biscuit aisle.
My friends back home will always love me.
I am proud of myself.

I don't know
how to not know.
I knew there were no classrooms -
only show and tell stages.

I show - not tell -
delusion.
I cannot believe
people let me believe
I belong here.

The girl who had to be
pretending for her safety
peers from behind me.

She stares at a girl in a lilac jacket
who looks like she doesn't know
how to not know.
Her notes are a beautiful pastel.

I sit beside her,
offering her a biscuit.

The game ends.

Her eyes snuggle
into my delusion
and tell her she's brilliant.

I hope we stay warm enough
to stop pretending.

Until then,

Would you like a biscuit?

learner

Dear learner driver,

Slow down.
Slow
Down.
Feel free to stall.
Bay park. Miss the bay.
Touch the kerb now and then.

Scowl at me all you want.

What if
you're not supposed to know how to parallel
park?
It's okay if you knocked over three bins when
you first tried.
Really.

Yelling does not undo mistakes.
Tell your teacher that.

You're allowed to breathe at junctions.
Rolling back on vertical climbs is allowed.
Grabbing your teacher's knee instead of the
gearstick?
More common than you know.

Hands that have trembled
since the moment they felt earth
can learn how to move,
slow and steady.
Ignore when they say
you have grown up too fast
to be driving so slow.

Will you learn to be brutal -
Will you pass their test?
Will you become a cat
chasing a rat's tail
screaming 'amber means go!'
How dare they turn left
when you want them right;
That anger of yours
needs someone to bite.
You only get angry
at someone you have never been -

        - right?

mister moribund's taxi

They say life is best observed
sat down.

In the driver's seat
of a taxi,
floating around the town.

Mister Moribund knew this to be true,
as he drove around
the autumn sundown.
Knowing where someone
was going
told him their story.

Noticing what they carried
told him their heart.

There was not a car
safer, or more comfy.
Mister Mori left pillows and blankets -
The journey often leaves us sleepy.

Mori opened his doors,
bound to his seat,
never quite ready for
who he was to meet.

Mothers begged to see their daughters,
cake trays on their knees.
Girlfriends giggled addresses,
stumbling together, in glee.
A child requests a kennel,
leaving the faint smell of treats.
An older man entered before him,
quiet, ready,
at peace.

Mori is never surprised by
the events in his backseat -
but his heart still plunges
and his hands tighten around his wheel
when an unexpected hand
waves from the street.

In walks a girl.
She is young,
and not afraid.
Mori cannot look her
in the eye.

He asks her shamefully
where he needs to stop by.
Her trembles sound tired,
her voice is deadly and dry.

She carries nothing.
Nothing solid.
Mori ignores the dripping sound.

He slows down
to grab her hand.
(he wishes his hands were cold.)
She begs to go;
Mori hesitates,
then loosens his hold.

'You can only get into a taxi
if you have a destination.'

She wails that she does.
She swears that she does,

but the taxi is still.

A slightly ajar window
catches Mori's eye,
without a rattling sound.
It lets in a lively chill.
He sighs.

'My, I'm going to run out of petrol.'

She laughs in response,
her lungs limp and tatty.

Mister Mori smiled.
His backseat felt
pleasantly empty.

'Oh, young girl.
what a gift it is;
having nowhere to be.'

The girl sat for a while.
She gazed out the window,
shyly yearning.

"We'll meet again, won't we?"
The girl asked carefully.

'Not in a hurry.
Breathe 'till then, dear.
It's a beautiful day for a walk.'
Mori winked.

And that it was.

suncatchers

I look at rain differently.
I gaze up at her fall
like a worried mother.

I wonder if she knows
meeting us is often met
with tuts and grunts.

The girl who reads books under trees
will not read today.
The birds will not be fed
by the man who wanders the square.
He'll be lonely today.
The girls in their new heels
will curse her today.

I wonder if
she means to make the world grey.

Does it make her want to hide
or become a storm?
Do her parents hear her sobs from next door?
Is the weight of a seventeenth birthday
too heavy to hold?

Or,
Is she too busy watching the grass grow?

I hold out my palm
and she wails through my fingers.
I wish I could tell her about puddles
and movie kisses
and races down car windows
and raincoats that look like ducks.
I wish to tell her
she is allowed
to be loud.

I sit beside her
with my pen,

As we both keep trying to grow flowers in grey
skies.

my friend, silence

She entered the room
and shut the door
quietly
behind her
while my best friend continued
to draw.

I welcomed her in,
my leg bouncing.
I inhaled an armour
for her heaviness -
I have met her before.
I knew she came swollen
and drenched
and guilty.

Today
she wasn't wearing her big coat.
She sat beside me
and we watched my best friend scribble.

'Magic, is it not?' she whispered
and placed her hand over mine.
we gazed in awe at my best friend's
dancing hands,

the way her tea cup kissed her dimple,
the way her mind wandered
in peace.

Everything I'd missed
had been so beautiful.

I looked at the stranger I once knew
in the eyes.
"You, my friend, are lovely."

That day, I thanked my two friends.
They asked me why.
I couldn't think of a reason,
so this is me trying.

Everything begins with a timid, little try.

leo's lullaby

Your name rolls off the tongue
like it was meant to be spoken.
Lee-oh. The closest name to love,
but sweeter. It bounces.

Ruler of the sun,
filling up cups until wounds fall undone,
you cradled my tears
from nineteen years

With sweetness intentional,
a strength so incredible,
everything so terrible
suddenly invisible
you,
star regulus,
satellite of joy.

In every life,
find me between July twenty third
and August twenty second
and sit with me
for a little longer each time.

sweet potato fries

Love is a deliberate coincidence.

My friends burst into my home
As soon as I begin making
sweet potato fries.

We roll up our sleeves
and peel potatoes together.
I cut them too many fries
and they reply
'we love you, too.'

The oven hums sweetly
and we dance, like friends do.
Tell me about your day
as you twirl under my arm.

Love found me on purpose.
I never happen to have
extra sweet potatoes
by accident.

Caring for you
is no coincidence.
I love you knowingly.

mama bear's bed

If Goldilocks wandered into my home
and ate my food
and slept in my bed?

I would leave a hair tie on the table
and sneak a hot water bottle
into the covers.

I would pour her tea
using the same kettle she scratched.
We can sit by the rain
by the same window she smashed.

She will not learn not to
smash windows
by watching me smash windows.

Her heart will know how to make
shadow puppets
and glow in the dark stars
and blankets with needles.
She will know
not to let the world make her sharp.
She will know.

The soul that is glazed over
like freshly-cut glass,
Listen.
Be soft,
let life melt you.
Others must know it is an honour
to hold your tender.
Waking up is always worth
shedding tears
because sunlight is dancing through the curtains
and there is a hair tie on the table.

untied laces

I smashed a glass tonight.
It shimmers on the carpet, in splinters.
The red wine
hides in the beige carpet's veins.
Those colours together always
gives me a fright.

It's more than an accident.
It grits its teeth and calls me vile.
Difficult.
Taxing.
Embarrassing.
It is a dreadful reminder of
who I forget
I am.

I hold my limbs close.
I cover my ears.
I am ready to flinch,
wince,
and run.

But there is no noise.
No one leaves.

We are in our kitchen

and you are giggling about
the carpet bleeding
and neither of us are wearing pants
and being safe
is so ridiculous
I have to laugh.

A sad sorry
sits on my tongue.
You say one of the shards
is shaped like a seagull,
and I hesitate.
You kiss my cheek
in knowing.

How lucky am I
to be so clumsy,
leaving my shoelaces untied
to fall to a pair of feet
so gentle, so sweet

Someone to show me
there is love in the broken,
in the undone,
in the messy.
Every single shard of me,
all of the time,
is loved.

With or without pants on.

37

that coffee date I promised

It's hot chocolate.

I already know what's swirling
in your mug
when I spot you,
sitting in the corner booth.

We hug.
I feel how your t-shirt is
tucked in
far too tight.
You leave your hands on my shoulders
like you used to.
Your hair looks longer. Lighter.
Both of our postures
are still terrible.

I ask how you've been.
Your mother's doing fine.
You like black coffee now,
and have stopped watching cartoons.

We laugh, and it sounds afraid.
An itchy softness.
I nearly blurt
'Why can't we forgive each other?'

It scratches the surface.
You look at me, horrified
when I tell you I still prefer
the cartoon Peter Pan.

You tell me I haven't changed.
I ask about you again,
because how can I say
you've made my thoughts nastier
and my words kinder?

Our talks drift in and out,
smoothly, like grit.
You don't offer to walk me home.

But I will remember you fondly.

Even though, even though, even though.

yours

Snuggle in, sweet love.
Leave everything that caused your heart to weep
and lose sleep
and landed you on the bathroom floor
at the front door. You don't need to carry it now.
The kettle's on - let me take your coat.

Our coats can feel ever so heavy.

Rest your eyes here.
I hope your days smell of the first rainfall in
autumn,
and your feet feel the satisfaction of a leaf
crunch with every step.
I hope your ears only hear love
and the melody of midnight laughter.
May your eyes see love in pain;
May they brim with love's water at the sight of
spring's first daffodils.
May your lungs rest steady, four and six,
may your heart never beat and punch your body,
may it only pulse with life, with you.

Someone will ask you
what your favourite feature of yours is,

and you will swell
as there are so many to choose from.

It will ease, dear reader.
It will ease.

up, up and away

I am a balloon animal,
who is free to fly to the moon.

Up, up and away.

I was made for other's smiles alone.
But my smile is warmer when I'm alone.

Up, up and away.

My paws swim in the starlight,
forever free of the tangle I used to be.

Up, up and away.

I lived nightmares to be
a girl who dreams.
I dream of visiting venus,
and learning how to love.
I dream of the world's arms
being open.
I dream of kittens, marigolds,
slow dancing in my kitchen.
My heavy mind will go,
to let my dreamer heart grow.

Up, up and away.

revelation 10:9

Leaving so soon?

Let me catch my breath, first.

My apologies.

I was terribly busy
locking a bathroom door.

Before you go,
indulge me.
Hear one last tale,
the best one.

This tale moves so fast
these days.
I cannot catch it
through words.

I have tried,
and failed.

Besides,
My words have other worries.
I like to believe they found themselves

in a stranger's arms,
snuggled into blankets.
Or with coffee,
on buses,
left behind in old apartments.

They have made a friend,
if I'm lucky.

Ah, I digress.
This story is not about me anymore.
Listen with care.

There is tomorrow,
and in tomorrow,
you will be.

Hold on!
The best is yet to come.

There you will be,
along with me.
what this tomorrow holds for us,
we both cannot wait to see.

Be here,
and please stay.
The best part is still on its way.